W9-BGU-503

Reducing and Recycling Waste

Jen Green

Published in 2012 by Windmill Books, LLC
303 Park Avenue South, Suite #1280, New York, NY 10010-3657

First Edition

Editor: Katie Powell
Designer: Stephen Prosser
Maps and Artwork: Peter Bull Art Studio
Sherlock Bones Artwork: Richard Hook
Consultant: Michael Scott, OBE

Library of Congress Cataloging-in-Publication Data

Green, Jen.
Reducing and recycling waste / by Jen Green. — 1st ed.
        p. cm. — (Sherlock Bones looks at the environment)
Includes bibliographical references and index.
ISBN 978-1-61533-382-0 (library binding : alk. paper)
1. Waste minimization—Juvenile literature. 2. Recycling (Waste, etc.)—Juvenile literature. I. Title.
TD792.G74 2012
363.72'8—dc22

2010048601

Photographs:
Cover © Louise Murray/Robert Harding, title page © Istock recycling glass (repeat p21), imprint page
© Image Works/TopFoto (repeat p27), 4 © Shutterstock, 5 © John Miller/Robert Harding, 6 © Wayland,
7 © ullsteinbild/TopFoto, 8 ©Louise Murray/ Robert Harding, 9 ©Thomas Schmitt/Image Bank/Getty Images,
10 © Wayland, 11 © Prashanth Vishwanathan/Reuters/Corbis, 12 © John Cancalosi/Still Pictures, 13 ©Wayland,
14 © Ray Roberts/Ecoscene, 15 © Construction
Photography/Corbis, 16 © Chris O'Reilly/
naturepl.com, 17 © Shutterstock, 18 © Sally
Morgan/Ecoscene, 19 © moodboard/Corbis,
20 © Franz-Peter Tschauner/dpa/Corbis, 21 © Istock
recycling glass (repeat p1), 22 © Mireille Vautier/
Alamy, 23 © Chinch Gryniewicz/ Ecoscene, 24 © Ian
Harwood/Ecoscene, 25 © Blend Images/Alamy, 26
© Burke/Triolo Productions/Getty Images, 27 © Image
Works/TopFoto (repeat p2), 28 © Liquid Light /Alamy,
29 © Chris Sattlberger/Photoconcepts/Corbis

Manufactured in China

For more great fiction and nonfiction,
go to www.windmillbooks.com

CPSIA Compliance Information: Batch # WAS1102WM:
For Further Information contact Windmill Books, New York, New York at 1-866-478-0556

Contents

🐾 Words that appear in **bold** can be found in the glossary on page 30.

The Environment Detective, Sherlock Bones, will help you learn about reducing and recycling waste. The answers to Sherlock's questions appear on page 31.

Why Is Waste a Problem?

Every day, every one of us produces waste, from candy wrappers to magazines and old batteries. But our waste is a problem to get rid of. What kinds of waste have you thrown away today?

Dealing with waste is called waste **disposal**. In most countries, **local authorities** are responsible for waste disposal. Many places have a weekly garbage collection. But the garbage collected from our homes still has to be disposed of somehow, so it doesn't harm the environment.

Every year there are more and more people in the world. That means more and more garbage! Waste disposal is expensive and uses energy and **resources**. On the bright side, a lot of what we throw away isn't really garbage at all—it includes all kinds of valuable materials that can be used again.

The garbage truck collects our trash each week. Waste disposal is funded by local taxes. Find out about garbage collection in your area—what is collected and how often?

DETECTIVE WORK

Use a scale to weigh the bagged trash your family throws away each week. Divide it by the number of people in your family, and then by seven, to find out how much trash each person throws away in a day. In some areas, trash cans are fitted with electronic tags so you can log onto a web site to check the weight of the waste you throw out.

🐾 **Can you think of a way of figuring out the weight of trash your family produces in a year?**

Waste that is dumped damages the natural world, such as this beach in the Dominican Republic.

Waste disposal is a major challenge across the world today. Luckily, we can all help to tackle the problem of waste by following the "three Rs"—**reduce, reuse, and recycle**. Everyone can reduce the volume of waste by creating less of it in the first place. Reuse is about using things again. Recycling is when waste materials, such as paper, metal, and plastic, are remade into new products. This book will explain about the "three Rs" and how they help to make a cleaner, greener world.

ECO-FACTS

How Much Waste?

In the United Kingdom, everyone throws away about 3.3 pounds (1.5 kg) of waste a day. In the United States, the figure is higher—about 4.6 pounds (2.1 kg). Some types of trash, for example, packaging from supermarkets, are actually lighter than they were 25 years ago. But a lot more goods are now packaged, so there's a greater volume of waste.

What Exactly Is Waste?

There are many different kinds of waste. As well as household trash, schools, farms, factories, offices, hospitals, and power plants all produce waste. Some types of waste are dangerous. They have to be disposed of carefully, so they don't damage the environment.

Every family in the country produces at least a trash can-full of garbage each week. A lot of what we throw away is either leftover food or food packaging, such as bottles, cans, and plastic containers. We also throw away worn-out clothes, toys, and machinery, and a lot of paper and cardboard. Large items such as old furniture and machinery have to be taken to the local dump.

We all flush lots of waste down the toilet, too, including some that really should go in the trash can. But remember that what goes down the toilet doesn't disappear. It is just another kind of waste that needs to be treated and disposed of, without damaging the planet.

This diagram shows the percentage of each type of waste found in the average trash can.

🐾 **Which types of waste do we throw away most of?**

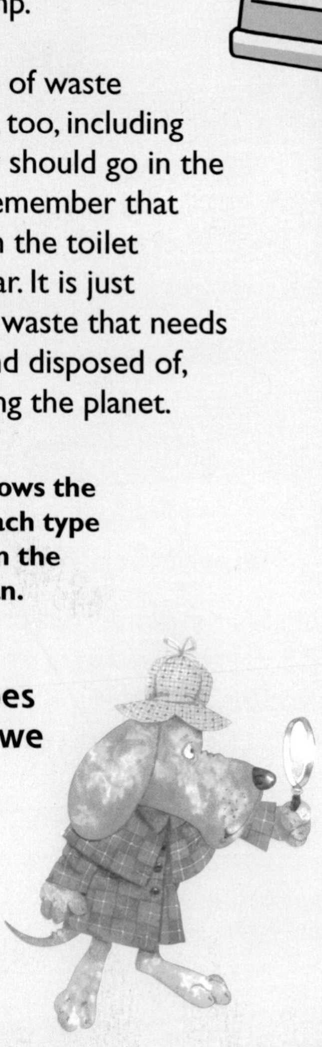

DETECTIVE WORK

Investigate exactly what goes in the trash can each week by sorting garbage into separate plastic bags. You will need six bags—for glass, metal, plastic, food waste, cloth, and paper/cardboard. Always wear gloves when touching garbage. At the end of the week, weigh each bag. Which type of waste is the heaviest? Which is the bulkiest?

Kitchen waste: 30%

Other, including clothes: 12%

Metal: 10%

Glass: 10%

Plastics: 8%

Paper and cardboard: 30%

ECO-FACTS

Nuclear Waste

Coal- and oil-burning power stations produce air pollution. Nuclear power plants produce even more dangerous waste as they process a fuel called uranium. Uranium gives off invisible **radiation** that can kill people and wildlife. This waste remains harmful for thousands of years.

Industry, business, and agriculture all produce waste, including used chemicals and old equipment. Waste can include liquids and gases as well as solid garbage. If liquid waste from farms and factories leaks into the natural world, it causes **pollution**. Factories and power plants release air pollution as they process **raw materials** and burn **fuel** for energy.

Some types of waste are **toxic**—poisonous. Toxic waste is particularly harmful if it enters the environment, so it has to be disposed of very carefully. For instance, hospital waste includes used needles and swabs that could be dangerous or spread diseases. Some factories produce chemicals that could explode. Homes need to get rid of toxic waste, too. Batteries, paint, bleach, and many cleaning products contain harmful chemicals. Your local authority can tell you how to deal with these things safely.

Scientists haven't figured out how to dispose of nuclear waste, so most of it is sealed in special containers like these and buried underground.

What Happens to Waste?

All the waste we throw away has to be disposed of somehow. Most is either buried, dumped, or burned. The rest is recycled, which is best for the environment. Fortunately, the amount of waste that is being recycled is increasing in countries around the world.

Most of the garbage we throw away is buried in pits called **landfills**. Some of these are old quarry workings, but many are dug specially. The **refuse** brought by truck, train, or **barge** is squashed down by bulldozers, then covered with soil to keep pests away. When the pit is full, a thick layer of soil is added. Then the site can be planted with grass and shrubs. Some old landfill sites are made into parks or golf courses, but we can't build on them because of the dangerous garbage beneath.

DETECTIVE WORK

Find out the locations of landfill sites in your area using the Internet, a library, or by contacting the local authority. Does garbage arrive by truck, train, or barge? Are any new landfill sites or **incinerators** planned in your area?

In the United States, about three-quarters of all waste ends up in landfills.

One of the problems is that many countries are running out of places to dump trash. Most people don't want a dump or landfill site in their neighborhood, and we can't afford to use up good farmland. We have to find new ways of getting rid of waste.

Some garbage is burned in furnaces called incinerators. Garbage can be used as fuel. The heat given off can be used to work machines called **turbines**, which produce electricity. However, burning trash can cause harmful pollution. The incinerator has to reach a very high temperature to burn materials such as plastics safely, otherwise toxic chemicals may be given off. Incinerators also produce a lot of ash that has to be buried in landfills.

When garbage is burned in an incinerator, waste gases are given off. Filters are fitted to chimneys to reduce pollution.

Not in My Backyard

Dumps and landfill sites can produce dust and smells that harm the local environment. Rumbling garbage trucks and trains can be noisy. These sites may also attract pests such as rats and mice, which can spread diseases. For these reasons, people don't want to live near a dump or landfill. Incinerators aren't popular either, because of the risk of pollution.

Who Produces Waste?

Waste disposal is a worldwide problem, but not all countries produce the same amount of garbage. People in more developed countries produce much more waste than those in the developing world.

In more developed countries, every family produces enough waste to fill their home in less than a year! A lot of what we throw away is packaging—the wrapping on food, toys, machinery, and other products. Packaging helps to protect the goods we buy. It also makes things look attractive, so we are more likely to buy them. But as soon as we get home, most packaging goes in the trash.

DETECTIVE WORK

Next time your family goes shopping, investigate the amount of packaging used on different foods, especially items such as cakes and chocolates. What products have the most layers of packaging? What items have the least?

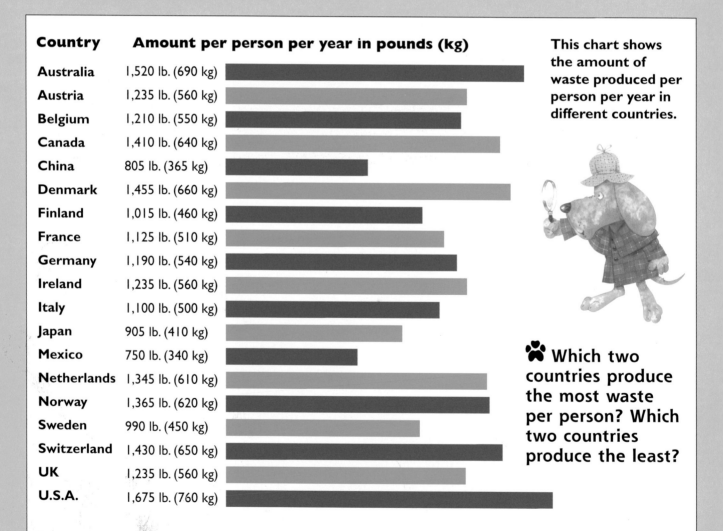

Country	Amount per person per year in pounds (kg)
Australia	1,520 lb. (690 kg)
Austria	1,235 lb. (560 kg)
Belgium	1,210 lb. (550 kg)
Canada	1,410 lb. (640 kg)
China	805 lb. (365 kg)
Denmark	1,455 lb. (660 kg)
Finland	1,015 lb. (460 kg)
France	1,125 lb. (510 kg)
Germany	1,190 lb. (540 kg)
Ireland	1,235 lb. (560 kg)
Italy	1,100 lb. (500 kg)
Japan	905 lb. (410 kg)
Mexico	750 lb. (340 kg)
Netherlands	1,345 lb. (610 kg)
Norway	1,365 lb. (620 kg)
Sweden	990 lb. (450 kg)
Switzerland	1,430 lb. (650 kg)
UK	1,235 lb. (560 kg)
U.S.A.	1,675 lb. (760 kg)

This chart shows the amount of waste produced per person per year in different countries.

❀ Which two countries produce the most waste per person? Which two countries produce the least?

In more developed countries, we live in a "throw-away society." Many of the things we buy aren't made to last. When equipment becomes faulty, it is often difficult to repair, so many people just buy a new one. Manufacturers encourage us to throw away items such as cell phones every year or so, and buy the latest model. All this creates a lot of waste. On the positive side, developed countries usually have strict laws on pollution, and they have the money to spend on the safe disposal of waste.

Less developed countries produce much less waste per person. In places such as India and Africa, most people can't afford to buy new things all the time, so used goods, from old shoes to cars, are carefully repaired. Materials such as cardboard, metal, and plastic are seen as valuable, so instead of being thrown away, they are recycled. However, there may also be less money to spend on waste disposal. In some countries, waste piles up on the streets or collects in dumps.

ECO-FACTS

Waste Pickers

In many less developed countries, recycling is a major industry. People known as **waste pickers** sort through garbage dumps to collect materials that can be sold for reuse or recycling. However, this work is dirty and can be dangerous.

In less developed countries, some people make a living sorting and selling materials for recycling. This man is collecting garbage in Mumbai, India.

How Does Waste Cause Pollution?

Waste that is just left lying around instead of being disposed of properly causes pollution. This includes litter, dumped furniture, and machinery, and also waste liquids and gases. Different kinds of waste can **pollute** the air, water, or soil.

When people dump waste on the street or in the countryside, it is called illegal dumping or **fly dumping**. Fly dumping is against the law in most countries, but trash is still dumped illegally. Fly dumping and litter can harm wildlife. For instance, animals and birds can get trapped in plastic, or be injured by metal or glass.

This stork has become trapped in a plastic bag. Without rescue, it could suffocate or die of starvation.

DETECTIVE WORK

Conduct a litter survey in a shopping mall or a park. Are enough trash cans provided in the area? Are the trash cans full, or has litter just been dropped carelessly? What types of litter are causing the problem? You could make a map of the site showing litter "hot spots," then contact your local authority and ask them to clean it up.

For years, people used the oceans as a giant trash can. All sorts of harmful waste was regularly dumped in the sea, where it poisoned **marine** life. Waste including **sewage** and chemicals from farms and factories has also been dumped in rivers for centuries. Fortunately, many countries now have laws that restrict the dumping of waste in rivers and the sea.

Dumps and landfill sites can pollute the air, soil, and water. If the site is not properly constructed, polluted water called **leachate** can seep into the surrounding soil and **contaminate** local water supplies. Nowadays, most landfill sites are lined with a layer of clay or plastic that prevents leachate escaping. Rotting garbage also gives off gas, which can produce a fire hazard. Today, this gas is often collected using a network of pipes. It may then be burned.

ECO-FACTS

Accidents at Dumps and Landfills

In 1993, gas seeping from a landfill site in Turkey caught fire and exploded. The explosion showered rotting refuse on nearby houses. In 2000, a large garbage dump in the Philippines collapsed, killing 300 people who were sifting through the waste.

This diagram of a landfill site shows safety features that help to prevent pollution.

🐾 **Look at the diagram. What safety features help to prevent waste polluting the air, water, and soil?**

Gas given off by rotting garbage is drawn off by pipes

Garbage cells

Soil layer

Drainage layer

Plastic liner

Layers of sand and gravel help prevent pollution but allow gas and water through

Leachate collection pipe

Why Reduce, Reuse, and Recycle?

The huge amounts of garbage we throw away each week are building up to harm the planet. Existing waste disposal sites are filling up and new ones are unpopular. The real waste is that much of what we throw away could be reused or recycled, to save resources and reduce pollution and waste.

We can all ease the problem of waste disposal and help the environment by reducing, reusing, and recycling—in that order. First, you can reduce the amount of waste by only buying what you need, when you need it. Do you really need the latest model? Can you share a book or game with a friend or family member? Choosing items with less packaging also reduces waste.

The range of materials that can be recycled depends on cost and also on whether there is a demand for them. Materials have to have some value for them to be worth the effort and cost of recycling.

ECO-FACTS

Curbside Collections

In many countries, materials for recycling are now collected from outside people's houses. Curbside collections encourage more people to recycle. They also save on the fuel used to make individual trips to **recycling centers**. Some of the money raised from selling recycled materials pays for the collection.

Items such as paper, glass, and plastic can often be reused rather than thrown away. For example, you may be able to return empty bottles and egg cartons for refilling. Can faulty equipment be repaired instead of being replaced? Items that cannot be reused can usually be recycled. This is when materials such as cardboard, metal, and plastic are reused either to make the same thing or a different product. A huge range of materials can now be recycled. Recycling reduces the raw materials that are taken from the environment and the energy used in manufacturing. This cuts pollution and reduces waste.

Modern recycling plants have machines that can sort many different materials, rather than being sorted by hand.

DETECTIVE WORK

Find out about different attitudes to recycling by asking among your friends and family. What do people think of the recycling facilities in your area? Are they in favor of recycling? Record the results in two columns, for and against recycling. Ask people to explain why they are for or against. You could make a chart to show the results.

What Kinds of Waste Rot?

Some types of garbage rot much more quickly than others. Natural, or **organic** materials, such as paper, wool, and leftover food, rot quickly. **Man-made** materials, such as plastic, glass, and metal, **decay** very slowly or not at all. This makes man-made materials very useful for storage and building purposes, but causes a problem when they are thrown away.

In the natural world, dead plants and animals rot quite quickly. Small or **microscopic** life forms, such as beetles, worms, fungi, and bacteria, break down dead animals, leaves, and wood. The **nutrients** in organic matter return to the soil and **nourish** plant growth, which provides food for animals. This natural form of recycling goes on all the time.

Without the work of nature's recyclers, such as insects and fungi, woodlands like this one would be covered by a thick layer of natural waste.

ECO-FACTS

Rates of Rotting

Fruit and vegetable peelings take about three months to rot. Paper takes a month; wool and cloth take 1–2 years. Metal cans take 100–300 years to decay. Plastic takes longer, about 450 years. Glass does not rot.

The garbage we dump in landfills rots more slowly. This is partly because it contains plastic and other man-made materials, but also because landfill sites are sealed and kept as dry as possible to avoid pollution from leachate. Waste that is dry and sealed from the air rots more slowly than waste in the open. Thirty-year-old newspapers have been dug up from landfill sites. Paper usually rots quickly, but these newspapers could still be read!

Rotting organic matter has many uses. Farmers spread manure and crop waste on their fields to act as **fertilizer**. The gas produced by rotting garbage in landfill sites can be burned as fuel to produce electricity. Some local authorities collect organic waste to make compost, which they then sell locally for people to use as fertilizer for their gardens. You could use fruit and vegetable peelings to make your own garden **compost** heap. Find out how to make one on page 28.

Litter washed up on the beach is mostly made up of man-made materials that don't rot and decay very slowly. Take a look the next time you visit the beach.

DETECTIVE WORK

Test different materials to find out how quickly items rot. You will need five plastic pots, soil, and five small items of trash, such as an apple core, a scrap of newspaper, a plastic toy, a candy wrapper, and a metal screw or paper clip. Bury each item in a different pot and label it. After a few months, dig up the contents to find which have rotted and which items have stayed the same. Use a trowel and a pair of gloves.

Arrange these materials in the order they take to rot, fastest to slowest: plastic milk carton, banana skin, metal soda can, woolen scarf.

How Can We Reduce, Reuse, and Recycle Paper?

Every day, we throw out huge amounts of paper. Paper and cardboard make up at least a third of all the garbage in landfill sites. Yet these are among the easiest materials to reuse and recycle. It's also easy to reduce paper waste.

Paper is made of wood from trees such as pine and spruce. At the paper mill, the **timber** is shredded into wood chips, which are mixed with water to make **pulp**. Bleach is added to produce white paper. The water then drains off and the pulp is pressed, rolled into sheets, and dried. Making paper takes energy and uses a lot of water. It creates air and water pollution. It also takes a lot of trees—40 percent of all timber is used to make paper. But then a lot of paper is quickly thrown away.

Paper mills use huge amounts of water, so they are often built close to rivers. They also cause water pollution.

ECO-FACTS

Paper for Recycling

Almost any type of paper can be recycled, including newspapers, magazines, cardboard packaging, wrapping paper, and egg cartons. Tissues and waxed paper shouldn't be recycled. Many different products can be made from recycled paper, including notebooks, stationery, wrapping paper, and toilet paper.

You can reduce paper waste by asking the post office not to have **junk mail** delivered to your home. Sending emails rather than notes or letters saves paper. Many offices and businesses are working toward being paper-free. Paper can also be reused. Always write or print on both sides of the paper. Unwrap presents carefully so you can reuse wrapping paper. Reuse envelopes by sticking a label over the address. Christmas and birthday cards and pictures from magazines can be made into new cards or gift tags.

Paper is recycled using a process similar to making paper from wood. Used paper and card are shredded, pulped, and then pressed, rolled, and dried. However, paper can only be recycled a limited number of times, because the fibers get shorter each time paper is pulped. Making paper from recycled materials saves 40 percent of the energy used to make new paper, and causes less pollution. It also saves trees, forestland, and woodland life.

This vehicle is lifting bales of recycled paper into a truck. The bales will be taken to a paper mill. One ton of recycled paper saves about 15 trees.

DETECTIVE WORK

Recycling symbols show products that are made from recycled paper. Other symbols indicate materials that can be recycled. Look for the symbols and try to buy recycled products.

Can Glass Be Reused and Recycled?

Glass is a very useful material that has been made for hundreds of years. Glass does not rot, so waste glass is a problem to get rid of. However, like paper, glass can easily be reused and recycled.

Glass is made by heating sand, soda ash, and **limestone** in a furnace at around 2,730°F (1,500°C). The mixture becomes a hot liquid, which is poured into molds and shaped by blowing air through it. The mixture cools and hardens into glass. The **minerals** used to make glass have to be mined, which causes pollution. Pollution is produced during manufacturing, which also uses a lot of energy.

A German factory worker checks glass bottle production. Almost all glass bottles now contain some recycled glass.

DETECTIVE WORK

Find out where bottle banks are located in your area. The local authority web site may have details. Many stores have bottle banks. Use a map to figure out the quickest route from your house to a bottle bank, to save time and energy used in recycling. Better still, combine it with another trip.

Throwing glass away is a waste of energy and natural resources. We can reduce the amount of waste glass by reusing and recycling. In many countries, glass bottles can be returned and refilled. You pay a small deposit on the bottle, which is refunded when you return it. Bottles and jars can also be reused to hold flowers, candles, pencils, and pens.

Glass for recycling must be rinsed and sorted into three colors: clear, green, and brown. Tops and corks must be removed, and labels if possible. At the recycling plant, bottles and jars are smashed up, reheated, and remolded. The furnace does not have to be so hot, so recycling glass saves 40 percent of the energy used to make new glass. It also causes less pollution and saves minerals.

Glass can be recycled any number of times. Recycled bottles may be used to make more bottles. When a material is recycled to make the same thing, it is called **closed loop recycling**. Recycled glass is also used to make many other products, including bricks, tiles, and fiberglass for boats.

Glass is easy to recycle. Always return empty bottles to the bottle bank.

ECO-FACTS

Reusing and Recycling Internationally

Many European countries, Canada, and many U.S. states have schemes for returning glass bottles. The UK recycles 46 percent of its glass. Germany and the Netherlands recycle 80 percent. Switzerland comes out top with 91 percent.

Which country recycles more of its glass, the Netherlands or the UK?

Is Metal Easy to Reduce, Reuse, and Recycle?

Most of the metal that ends up in landfills comes from food and drinks cans. A light, flexible metal called **aluminum** is used to make drinks cans and also metal foil. Strong steel is used for food cans. These materials can easily be recycled, which reduces metal waste.

Metals come from rocks called **ores**. Aluminum is made from the mineral bauxite. Mining bauxite creates pollution and damages **habitats** such as rain forests. The ore is separated from the rock by melting it in a hot furnace. This process, called **smelting**, uses a lot of energy. It also produces air pollution and quantities of waste rock. Steel is made by smelting iron ore, charcoal, and limestone in a furnace.

This photo shows pollution around a bauxite mine in Brazil. The red mud, called slurry, is waste rock mixed with water.

DETECTIVE WORK

At the recycling center, metals are sorted using a powerful magnet. Steel is magnetic, aluminum is not. Test metals at home using a magnet. Are cans, coins, keys, and silverware magnetic? If they are, they are probably made of steel.

🐾 **What metal is used to make tinfoil? What metal are paper clips made of?**

Metal cans aren't that easy to reuse, but metal can easily be recycled. Food and drinks cans are expensive to produce, but new cans can easily be made from old ones. This makes recycling cans cost-effective. Drinks cans are one of the most commonly recycled materials.

At the recycling plant, aluminum cans are cleaned, squashed, melted, and molded into new cans—another example of closed loop recycling. Making cans from recycled aluminum saves 95 percent of the energy used making cans from new metal. It also cuts 95 percent of the pollution. Steel is also widely recycled. Steel cans are made into a wide range of products, from paper clips and silverware to cars, computers, and new food cans. Making cans from recycled steel saves 25 percent of the energy used making them from fresh steel.

This city farm in Perth, Australia, is collecting aluminum drinks cans for recycling to raise money for the farm.

ECO-FACTS

The First Cans

Metal cans were first used to preserve food about 200 years ago. The first cans were made of iron coated with a thin layer of tin—that's why they are called "tin cans." Many cans were once sealed with lead, but then people discovered lead was poisonous, so the use of lead in cans was banned.

Can Plastic Be Reused and Recycled?

Plastic is a fairly modern invention compared to metal. Plastic is strong and light. It can be thin and flexible, or thick and sturdy, which makes it incredibly useful. Plastic is used to make a huge range of products, including a lot of packaging. Plastic is also extremely long-lasting, which makes it a long-term waste disposal problem.

Plastic is made from oil—the world's most valuable fuel. Mining and transporting oil causes pollution, and the world's supplies of oil are limited. One day oil will run out, so it's important to **conserve** it, and not throw oil products away. About 8 percent of all oil is used to make plastic.

Plastic is used to package many food products, including fragile items such as fruit, vegetables, and eggs.

ECO-FACTS

Plastic Bags

Until very recently, plastic bags were given away free of charge by stores and supermarkets. Millions of bags ended up in landfill sites or blowing around the streets as litter. However, in the twenty-first century, there has been a drive to reduce this waste. Some stores have stopped giving the bags away, and many people now carry reusable cloth bags instead. You can also reuse plastic bags.

More and more plastic is thrown away each year. Plastic is **nonbiodegradable**—it lasts for hundreds of years, polluting the environment. We can reduce plastic waste by reusing plastic tubs and cups as containers. For example, ice creams tubs make great sandwich boxes. Yogurt cups can be used to grow seedlings or hold pens. You can wash and reuse plastic plates and cutlery.

There are many types of plastic, including polystyrene (foam packaging) and fabrics such as nylon. Some types can be recycled. A plastic called PET, used to make drinks bottles, can be recycled to make fleece jackets, clear packaging, and more plastic bottles. Other plastics are recycled to make clothespins, sleeping bags, drainpipes, waterproof boots, and wheeled trash cans. However, only about 10 percent of all plastics are recyclable. Other types end up in landfills, dumps, and incinerators to cause pollution.

Cloth shopping bags last much longer than plastic ones and are kinder to the environment.

DETECTIVE WORK

Today, thin plastic bags are often made so they **biodegrade** quickly. Investigate what happens if you leave a bag exposed to sunlight for a few months. Other plastic bags, such as potato chips bags, are nonbiodegradable. If you see a potato chips bag lying around as litter, look at the use-by date to see how old it is.

What Else Can I Reduce, Reuse, and Recycle?

Twenty years ago, almost all waste was either dumped or buried. Now clothes, books, batteries, mobile phones, computers and even Christmas trees can all be reused or recycled to reduce waste.

Your old clothes can be recycled to make new fabrics or stuff furniture. You can also take them to a thrift store, along with toys, games, and books. Some thrift stores take old stamps, furniture, china, records, and cell phones, too. You can also sell these things at a yard sale or school sale. Old-style batteries contain dangerous chemicals that have to be disposed of carefully. Now you can buy batteries that can be recharged from an electric socket. Stores that sell cell phones may be able to repair or recycle your old one. Some companies recycle computers. Even Christmas trees can be chipped for compost! Contact your local authority for more advice about reducing, reusing, and recycling.

Take your old books and toys to a thrift store or have a yard sale. Stuff you have grown out of or gotten bored with may be just right for someone else!

ECO-FACTS

Zero Waste

If you recycle paper, glass, plastic, metal, and all the other things mentioned on this page, there won't be a lot of garbage left for landfill! Some environmental campaigners are working toward "zero waste," when everything can be either reused, repaired, composted, or recycled. This goal is some way in the future, but the more we recycle, the more cost-effective recycling becomes.

YARD SALE

Cans, bottles, and cardboard can be recycled at school.

Schools are great places to reduce, reuse, and recycle waste. Ask your teacher if you can start a recycling scheme at school if there isn't one already. You may be able to raise money for new equipment, a school trip, or your favorite charity through recycling. You could also ask the school to buy recycled products such as paper and toilet paper.

Your class could start a campaign to get the whole school recycling. Encourage everyone to use both sides of the paper before recycling. Fruit peel and kitchen waste can go on the compost heap. You may be able to get a **grant** to buy large recycling containers or smaller paper ones for each classroom.

DETECTIVE WORK

Investigate what gets thrown away in the classroom. At the end of the day, sort the garbage in the trash can by material. Keep a tally of the numbers of each type of waste and add up the weekly totals. How much can be recycled?

Your Project

I f you've done the detective work and answered all of Sherlock's questions, you now know a lot about reducing, reusing, and recycling waste. Investigate further by producing your own project. You could choose from the following ideas.

Practical Action

- Start a compost heap at home or at school. In just a few months, food and yard waste will rot down to provide a rich compost for the grounds or garden. You can buy a compost bin from a gardening center. Or you can make one from a wooden packing crate or an old trash can with holes drilled in the base and sides.
- Dead leaves and flowers, moist shredded paper, and fruit and vegetable peeling can go on the compost. Don't compost meat, dairy products, or cooked food. Add a few shovelfuls of soil, and water the heap regularly in dry weather. Turn the compost with a fork every few weeks.

Topics to Investigate

- Compare what is being done to reduce, reuse, and recycle waste in two cities or countries in different parts of the world. Are waste disposal methods the same? What materials are reused and recycled? Which area has the best record of dealing with waste?
- Focus on one type of waste, such as paper, plastic, or metal, and find out more about how it is made, reused, and recycled.
- Find out more about litter and its effects on wildlife and the natural world.
- Find out more about reducing, reusing, and recycling waste using this web site: www.epa.gov/kids/garbage.htm

Your local library and the Internet can provide all sorts of information. When you have gathered the information for your project, you might like to present it in an interesting way, using one of the ideas on page 29.

In about six months, the compost will be ready to put on the garden.

Project Presentation

- Write a short story or poem about recycling from the point of view of a drinks can, glass or plastic bottle, or candy wrapper.
- Design a poster to explain the importance of the "three Rs" or why it is important not to drop litter. Or your class could produce an exhibition of art made from recycled materials.
- Ask your teacher if you can hold a class debate about the best way of tackling litter and waste.
- Imagine you are making a television documentary or writing a magazine article about waste and recycling. Write a plan showing the main points you want to talk about in the order that makes the most sense.

You can look after your local area or school by volunteering to pick up litter that has been left behind. Remember to always wear gloves!

🐾 Sherlock has found out about recycling pet food cans. He thinks that if all the pet food cans thrown away in a year were laid end to end, they would stretch all the way around the world!

Glossary

aluminum A strong, light silver-gray metal, made from a mineral called bauxite.

barge A flat-bottomed boat.

biodegrade To rot away naturally.

closed loop recycling When an item of waste is recycled to make the same product.

compost A fertilizer for plants made from rotted natural materials.

conserve To protect the natural world.

contaminate To pollute.

decay To rot.

disposal When people get rid of something.

fertilizer A natural or man-made chemical that helps plants to grow.

fly dumping The illegal dumping of waste.

fuel A substance that can be burned or used up to produce energy.

grant Money given from a public fund for a specific purpose.

habitat A place where particular types of plants and animals live, such as a desert or rain forest.

incinerator A hot furnace in which garbage is burned.

junk mail Mail that is not sent to a particular person, but delivered to many homes to advertise businesses.

landfill A large pit where garbage is packed down and covered with soil.

leachate Water contaminated by waste escaping from a landfill.

limestone A rock used in glass-making and for other uses.

local authority The organization that runs services such as waste collection and recycling in an area.

man-made Made by humans.

marine To do with the sea.

microscopic Something that cannot be seen by the naked eye but is seen through a microscope.

mineral A nonliving natural substance.

nonbiodegradable Of materials that do not rot.

nourish To provide with food or other substances for growth and well-being.

nutrient A substance that nourishes living things.

ore A metal-bearing rock.

organic Any material made from the natural products of plants or animals.

pollute When harmful materials dirty the air, water, or soil.

pollution Damage to the environment caused by chemicals or natural substances in too much quantity.

pulp A mixture of water and wood fibers.

radiation Rays. Material said to be radioactive gives off harmful rays.

raw material A natural material, such as wood or minerals, that is used in manufacturing.

recycle When garbage is saved and remade into a new product.

recycling center A place where waste materials are recycled.

reduce To make something smaller or use less of it.

refuse Another word for trash.

resource A useful material.

reuse When something is used again.

sewage Dirty water from homes, containing chemicals and human waste.

slurry A semiliquid mixture.

smelting When metal is extracted from rock by heating and melting.

thrift store A store that sells secondhand items to raise money for charity.

timber Wood used in factories and for building.

toxic Poisonous.

turbine A machine powered by steam, gas, or water that is used to generate electricity.

waste picker A person who sorts through garbage to find materials that can be reused or recycled.

Answers

Page 4: Multiply the weight of garbage your family throws away each week by 52 (the number of weeks in a year) to find out roughly the weight of trash in a year.

Page 6: Paper, cardboard, and kitchen waste make up about 60 percent of the contents of the average trash can before recycling.

Page 10: The United States and Australia produce the most waste per person of the countries listed. China and Mexico produce the least.

Page 13: Garbage is covered with soil or sand and gravel to keep pests away. Pipes draw off gas given off by rotting garbage. The liner prevents liquid waste from polluting the soil.

Page 17: Banana skin, woolen scarf, metal soda can, plastic milk carton.

Page 21: The Netherlands recycles more of its glass than the UK.

Page 22: Aluminum is used to make tinfoil. Metal paper clips are usually made of steel.

Further Reading and Web Sites

Books

Environment in Focus: Waste Management
by Cheryl Jakab
(Benchmark Books, 2010)

Green Team: Waste and Recycling
by Sally Hewitt
(Crabtree Publishing Company 2008)

Reduce, Reuse, Recycle!: Food Waste
by Jen Green
(PowerKids Press, 2010)

Saving Our Living Planet: Earth-Friendly Waste Management
by Charlotte Wilcox
(Lerner Publishing Group, 2008)

Web Sites

For Web resources related to the subject of this book, go to: http://www.windmillbooks.com/weblinks and select this book's title.

Index